the worst album covers in the world... EVER!

NEW HOLLAND

Contents

Brief History of the Album Cover

The album ruled the Earth, or at least the record store, for over 40 years. When the long-playing vinyl record, or LP as it is better known, was driven out by the compact disc in the late 1980s, much was said about the improved sound quality and portability of the new format; yet little was said about the loss of one of the most widespread forms of popular culture in the 20th century.

Music records started out in the 1920s as 10-inch, 78-rpm discs and were only 'singles', usually containing one song per side. They were sold in plain paper sleeves and the centre label on the record was the only artwork in evidence. Often, collections of discs by the same artist were sold in books or 'albums', but even these were unadorned apart from the simple printing on the spine or cover.

In 1939, 23-year-old Alex Steinweiss, the art director for Columbia Records, became convinced that record sales could be improved by adding some colour and design to the packaging. He spent months haggling with sceptical executives over the extra cost of such a wild idea. Finally, with the release of *Smash Song Hits* by the songwriting team Rodgers and Hart, the album cover was born!

Album covers have come a long way from the early days of simple paper sleeves.

Soon, record companies discovered that the cover design could make or break the sales of an album. By the time LPs arrived in the late 1940s, which enabled an entire album of 78s to be recorded on one sturdy, 12-inch disc, even record company executives realized that the value of having a good illustrated sleeve was as important to sales as the music itself.

As printing costs diminished and technology improved, the album cover evolved from simple text and graphic artwork to full-colour photography, conceptual design and, eventually, into a one-square-foot art form in its own right. New genres of recorded music emerged, each developing its own distinct cover style. In the 1950s, the designers of rock and R&B covers seemed content to show a simple photo of the artist, leaving album cover innovation for releases by orchestras and lounge singers, whose records of this era were known for their lurid photography and well-endowed models. By the late 1960s, rock'n'roll led the way, introducing politics, controversy and often an element of gimmickry to the album cover. Andy Warhol's peeling banana for *The Velvet Underground & Nico* and the Rolling Stones' zippered cover for *Sticky Fingers* were among the first 'interactive' album covers.

By the 1970s, the album was becoming increasingly more of a package deal, with designs often continuing onto the back covers and inner sleeves. Some cover designers felt too confined even by this and the 'gatefold' was invented, giving artists a few more square feet to work with. The pinnacle of gatefold art is perhaps Isaac Hayes's *Black Moses*, which has a two-sided, cross-shaped gatefold to allow a full 12-square-feet of album cover!

In the 1980s, many major label pop acts reverted to covers showing pictures of themselves, albeit with bigger hair. The creative forces of the recording industry had refocused on the music video, while new portable stereo systems drove increased sales of the cassette tape, despite the poor sound and shrunken cover art. The torch of album cover innovation was thus passed to small, independent labels, which took advantage of cheap printing and record pressing to create DIY classics.

Enter the compact disc. The sound was clean and clear and they could be played at home, in your car or from your hip. Launched in 1982, 53 million CDs were sold in the United States alone by 1986. Meanwhile, the familiar 12-inch squares seemed to many to be obsolete – 40-year-old relics that were doomed to moulder in boxes in the attic or be dumped in a local charity's donation bin. The age of the album was over.

Technology, however, comes with a price – the new 'album cover', the CD insert, was smaller, less detailed and hidden behind plastic. New releases featured artwork that was much less ambitious, while classic records that had been reissued on CD had their covers shrunk to fit. Your favourite old record might sound great on CD, but admiring the cover is a bit like watching an epic movie such as *Lawrence of Arabia* on television – it's just not the same!

However, the vinyl record has not disappeared completely. Stubborn 'audiophiles' continue to demand high-quality re-pressings of classic jazz, classical and rock records; the DIY punk-rock scene continues to use vinyl as a subversion of the corporate digitalization of music; and the greatest demand for new vinyl comes from the club DJ scene, as the ability to manipulate the speed and direction of a turntable creates sounds not easily reproduced in the digital realm. Unfortunately for the fan of cover art, the vinyl record has come full circle; most DJ records released today are singles sold in plain sleeves, just like the 78s of three-quarters of a century ago.

Collecting Forgotten Records

I consider myself a collector of 'forgotten' records. These aren't the ones you'll find displayed on the wall in the record shop, they're not listed in value guides usually and most record collectors don't even notice them. These are the records that remain in the sale box after everyone else has already rifled through it and bought the 'good' ones. Forgotten records can be found at junk shops, car-boot sales, flea markets and, if you're lucky, piled in the neighbour's rubbish after a clean out. You can try looking at your local second-hand record shop, but you'll have to go digging in the dusty boxes kept hidden under the counter. Just about anyone over the age of 30 has some records stashed somewhere. Ask your friends. If their records are kept in alphabetical order in plastic bags beneath the stereo, don't bother looking at them. However, if they vaguely recall seeing a box full of vinyl in the cellar years ago, you may have just found some forgotten records!

Collecting something no one else wants has its advantages. I rarely pay more than US$1 for a record. You can get up late and go to the sales after they've been 'picked over' and still find a gem or two. But the most satisfying thing I've found about collecting forgotten records is the thrill of discovering an artist who has toiled for years making discs, despite a complete lack of recognition for their efforts.

In a time when anyone with a microphone and a CD burner can put out their own 'record', it's important to remember that things were different in the days of vinyl. A person who thought their talent was too great to be kept silent had to first find a recording studio. After the performance was committed to tape, it had to be mixed and mastered before being

Second-hand and junk shops are often great sources of unwanted albums.

pressed onto vinyl. Meanwhile, a photographer had to be hired and the record sleeves printed. After you finally had your records in hand, there was still the problem of selling them! While there were some 'vanity' record labels who handled most of this work for you, it's safe to say that putting out a vinyl record on your own required no small amount of time, money and commitment.

So, who were the people behind these forgotten records? The internet, of course, is a great research tool. As I have tracked down some of these artists for my website and this book, I am continually amazed by what I have found. Some of these artists are quite well known in their particular field, be it polka or the pulpit. Many are still performing, seemingly unaffected by decades of obscurity. Others are complete mysteries; when my own website posting is the only result of an internet search for someone, I know I've found a truly forgotten record!

A Tour of Forgotten Records

What makes a good forgotten record? Unless you carry a turntable with you while shopping, your judgement will be mostly based on the cover. Sometimes the whole concept is strange, like 'Music to Grow Plants' (see page 59) or 'Carpet Square' (see page 53). Sometimes it's just the cover photo that seems too suggestive to have gone unnoticed by its creators, such as Dennis Farnon's *Caution! Men Swinging* (see page 31) or Eddie Layton astride his rocket (opposite). Often the

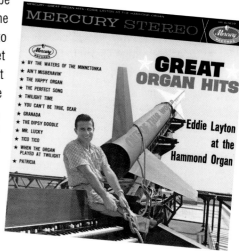

Eddie Layton's less than subtle 'organ' music covers ought to become the stuff of legend.

cover is amusing simply for the clothing and hairstyles worn by the artists. As many covers in this book demonstrate, anyone can mimic a current style, but it takes a true artist to create one that's all their own!

Any collector of forgotten records quickly notices just how many tend to be 'religious' recordings. This should be no surprise. The Christian music industry in the United States releases just about as many records as its secular cousin. Yet the vast majority of these records remain unknown outside the industry and unacknowledged by most record collectors. Although many Christian records may have been successful over the years, the majority of artists have motivations other than money or fame. As a result, we see many things that would never work in a more commercially motivated genre. The sheer number of different records released by Christian artists in the age of vinyl is staggering, and their great variety is the backbone of collecting forgotten records.

By far the most successful label in the Christian recording industry has been Word Records, located in Waco, Texas, where it still operates. Word's production values rival that of the major labels and many of their early cover designs are classics of the genre. The label released over 700 different titles from 1952 until 1974, when ABC purchased the company.

The number of records released by big Christian labels like Word, however, pales in comparison to those of the small labels and self-released endeavours. Because these were often made in small numbers and sold by the artists at their performances, it is an impossible task to track them all down. Although this book features many of this kind from my collection, there are countless more still out there waiting to be discovered!

Genres and Sub-Genres

Despite the endless variety of forgotten records to be found, after a while one begins to notice patterns, similarities and entire forgotten genres! Following are just a few examples of the kinds of records you may find.

PREACHERS AND SINGING FAMILIES

For many church leaders in the vinyl age, a chapel full of parishioners each Sunday was not enough. Their message was too important – there were thousands of lost souls wandering the world, just waiting to hear the word of God. Just about everyone had a phonograph player at home, so a great opportunity emerged for the small-time preacher to become a big-time soul winner. Like any entertainer in the latter half of the 20th century, having a record made a preacher 'legit'.

Often the preacher used this forum to tell his or her life story. Freddie Gage (see page 34), Gertrude Behanna, Jack Brown and dozens of others committed to vinyl their stories of a life of drugs, booze and sin left behind because of the love of Jesus. Other preachers seemed to have something of a competition going and used the back cover of their records as a kind of holy résumé: '4,000 souls won in 4 years as a travelling evangelist,' claims Reggie Thomas; '70,000 decisions made for Christ in the last 20 years,' says Dr Jack Van Impe; 'One million conversions in a single year,' trumps Chris Panos. Many of these preachers obviously had something of a business sense, too... The vinyl ministries of Jack Van Impe, Jimmy Swaggart, Jim Bakker and others evolved into multi-million dollar, tax-exempt enterprises that thrive to this day.

Another commonly seen religious phenomenon is the 'singing family' record. Little was needed for a small-town family to become big-time recording artists: just the song of Jesus in the heart, matching outfits in the closet, a last-minute stop for mother at the hair salon and a singing family was born! Many of these families took the show on the road to camp meetings and revivals throughout the southern United States. We know this because the tour bus is often prominently featured on the album cover. Some such groups were quite talented and went on to have successful gospel music careers, like the Happy Goodmans and the Blackwood Brothers. With others, a few copies of a single record album are all that remain to remind us of the family's foray into song.

Little Marcy was the puppet of ventriloquist Marcy Tigner. Tigner never quite perfected her act and would tell her young audiences that she was just singing along with Little Marcy when they noticed her lips moving!

Ventriloquist Records

Not all forgotten records are religious, of course. After a decade of digging though second-hand records, one notices some odd genres, or maybe sub-sub-genres, of music. Let's take ventriloquist records. If you think about it, the talent of 'throwing your voice' is a visual trick – in person it might be impressive, but when recorded and sent through a set of speakers… well, it's just somebody putting on a funny voice. Nevertheless, there have been a seemingly endless number of ventriloquist and puppet records released over the years. Some were instructional, such as Jimmy Nelson's classic *Instant Ventriloquism*. Others were extensions of children's television shows, such as Cadet Don and his alien sock-puppet Seymour from Houston, Texas. Of course there were Christian ventriloquist acts: Little Marcy is the best known (see page 79), but Geraldine and Ricky prove that she was no fluke. There were even a few 'adult' dummy acts, such as Rickie Layne's Velvel (see page 46) and the Spanish-language Oscar Zamora y Don Chema (see page 91).

Health and Fitness

There have been many attempts to promote fitness and health via the exercise record. *Jane Fonda's Workout Record* is one of the best-selling records of all time, as well as one of the records most often donated to charity shops! Before Jane, however, there was Bonnie Pruddin, who on *Fitness For Teens* cautions boys against girdled girls: 'If she has to be held together with rubber bands, she has made a poor start which can only get worse with each succeeding baby.' Debbie Drake takes over after marriage, whose checklist on *How to Keep your Husband Happy* (see page 29) goes beyond physical fitness to suggest that a wife should 'Be at home when he arrives... Nice voice (keep it soft and musical; also a pretty laugh)... Mentally alert (try reading).'

INSTRUCTIONAL RECORDS

Another very entertaining genre is the instructional record. When the 21st-century man wants to learn something new, he turns to the internet. Forty years ago, he would have turned to his hi-fi. Records were released giving advice about how to sell, how to fly, how to read minds, how to cook, how to type, how to garden – everything a man of the atomic age needed to know. The best of these records have plenty of 'enclosures', such as booklets, charts, quizzes and even packets of seeds. Did these records actually work? I'm not sure, but the longevity of some of their producers, such as the Success Motivation Institute (see page 44), shows that they must be doing something right.

'SPECIAL' ARTISTS

Another record genre that you'll often see is the 'very special' artist record. These days, political correctness demands that we all but ignore an individual's disability or medical condition. In the age of vinyl, artists had no problem exploiting their uniqueness to sell their records and their message. Merrill Womach, a struggling gospel singer, finally found success after being severely burned in a plane crash and covering his next record with graphic photos. Roy Thackerson, who was maimed as a child, invented a new method of playing to become the Fingerless Fiddler (see page 78). Meanwhile, the blind Brailettes,

Lowell Mason, aka The Singing Midget, made the most of his physical stature to separate himself from the crowd of other religious singers.

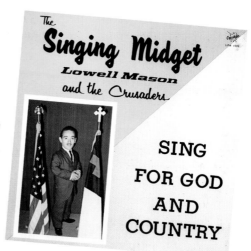

Lowell 'The Singing Midget' Mason (see page 71) and dozens of others used their conditions to offer a unique view of life, and make some great forgotten records in the process.

The Worst Album Covers... Ever!

This book is a sampling of what some have called 'the worst' covers from my forgotten-record collection. At the same time, of course, they are some of the best! The most shocking, the most mundane, the most ugly, the most incomprehensible... Are there more of the worst album covers out there waiting to be pulled from their dark hiding places? Undoubtedly! Forgotten records, even ones as bad – or good – as those in this book, are not particularly difficult to find. However, if you're looking for a *specific* record, you may be in for a long and fruitless search – there's no way of knowing how many of a particular record were originally made, let alone where they are now! But, at the end of the day, there's nothing stopping any of you from venturing out to a local junk shop, flea market or wherever forgotten records congregate in your area and starting a collection of your own. Have fun!

artist **101 STRINGS**

title **After a Hard Day – Music to Relax By**

The top easy listening string orchestra of all time, 101 Strings, never existed as such. Producer D.L. Miller hired various European orchestras on the cheap to make the recordings. Over the course of 45 years, the non-existent 101 Strings have recorded over 200 albums!

artist **ALVIS BARNETT AND THE BARNETTS**

title **If you don't believe we're real, Hide and Watch**

The Barnetts are 'Christian hippies' – while many young musicians in the 1970s expressed themselves through drugs and sex, others turned to Jesus. The results were often a bizarre combination of rebellion and religion. The Barnetts can be heard in the classic film, *Nashville*.

artist **JOE BATAAN**

title **Rap-O Clap-O**

Joe Bataan, aka Peter Nitollano, released this album in 1980. It was recorded, supposedly, prior to Sugarhill Gang's *Rapper's Delight*, making it arguably the first ever rap recording. In any case, it may well have been the *last* rap album without women or cars on the cover.

artist **DAVE BOYER**

title **Thank You Lord**

Here's a man who knows the value of a sharp suit, a beautiful family and, above all, a good dentist! Before finding God, Dave Boyer, aka Joey Stephens, was an Atlantic City lounge singer. He performed with the likes of Frank Sinatra and has been called 'The Lost Rat Packer'.

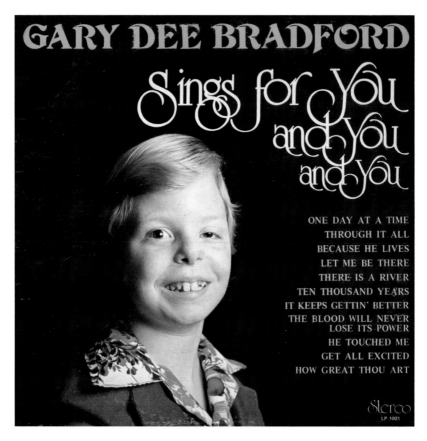

ONE DAY AT A TIME
THROUGH IT ALL
BECAUSE HE LIVES
LET ME BE THERE
THERE IS A RIVER
TEN THOUSAND YEARS
IT KEEPS GETTIN' BETTER
THE BLOOD WILL NEVER LOSE ITS POWER
HE TOUCHED ME
GET ALL EXCITED
HOW GREAT THOU ART

Stereo
LP-1001

artist **GARY DEE BRADFORD**

title **Sings For You and You and You**

Gary Dee Bradford from Baytown, Texas, was born without any arms. He released this, his first record, at the age of 11, and it paid for itself within just six weeks! Gary currently runs a music ministry and is an advocate for the disabled.

John Bult

Julie's Sixteenth Birthday

artist **JOHN BULT**

title **Julie's Sixteenth Birthday**

This is a simple cover, really: a grown man, a young girl, half a glass of beer, a forgotten cigarette. So, why is it so disturbing? Even though a listen to the record reveals that Julie is Mr Bult's daughter and she's about to go on her first date, it's STILL perturbing!

artist **MAX BYGRAVES**

title ***Viva! Congalongamax Vol. 10***

A versatile entertainer who rose to stardom starring opposite a ventriloquist's dummy in the BBC radio show *Educating Archie*, Max Bygraves became most famous for his television appearances and a series of *Singalongamax* records, among them this 1975 recording.

VISTEL SOUND
CORPORATION

STEREO

JESUS LOVES ME
Wayne Carr

SIDE ONE

TESTIMONIAL MEDLEY
(Softly and Tenderly, Everlasting
Arms, Power In The Blood)
SWEET JESUS
JESUS LOVES ME
SWEET HOUR OF PRAYER
EXODUS

SIDE TWO

OVER THE SUNSET MOUNTAINS
SHEPHERD OF LOVE
WHAT A FRIEND WE HAVE IN
JESUS
FILL MY CUP, LORD
IT IS NO SECRET (What God
Can Do)

artist **WAYNE CARR**

title **Jesus Loves Me**

Jesus may love Wayne, but it doesn't look like his tailor's such a fan
– yet again, another religious singer attempts to convert the masses
through music, style and charisma – and as for his parents... what
were they thinking of when they named him?

artist **THE CASTLE FAMILY**

title   **Love that Showbiz!**

In the wake of The Osmonds, family variety acts sprung up all over the United States. This happy-looking bunch hailed from Minneapolis, Minnesota. They apparently really do 'love that showbiz', because a recent check showed they were still performing.

artist **THE CENTURIANS**

title **Surfers' Pajama Party**

The cover notes provide surfers with some rules for a successful 'pajama' party: find a large house with a record player; find an old bathtub, fill it with ice and pour in any soft drink (which can later be spiked as required) and, of course, wear 'pajamas'!

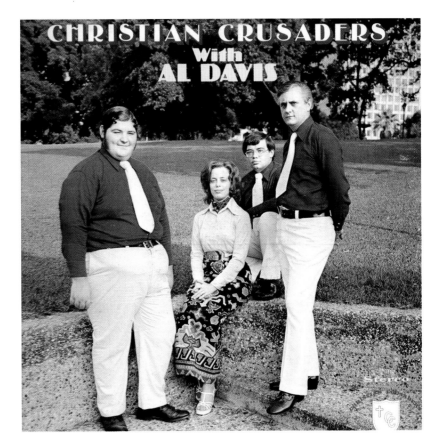

artist **CHRISTIAN CRUSADERS**

title **With Al Davis**

Many of these groups went to great lengths to wear matching outfits, but what's strange is how the *people* often don't seem to match. Where else would you see this motley crew other than on a Christian album cover?

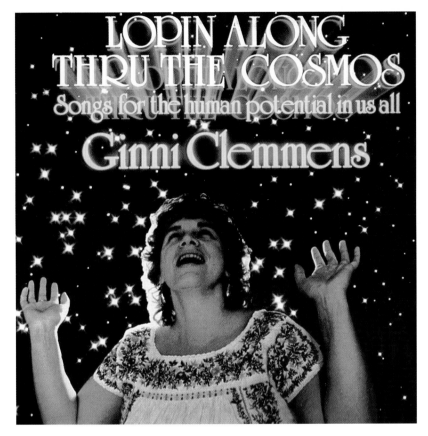

artist **GINNI CLEMMENS**

title **Lopin Along Thru the Cosmos (Songs for the human potential in us all)**

Ginni was a founding member of the Chicago folk music scene in the 1950s and '60s and became an important figure in 'women's music'. Surely this must be the only album ever released with 'lopin' in its title?

artist **THE COOPER FAMILY**

title **I'm God's Child**

The Cooper family is a proud family: proud of the kids, proud of Mom's sewing skills and quite proud of their fireplace. This does not explain, however, the framed medieval weapons on the wall, although the Cooper Family does hail from Texas.

artist **DON COSTA'S FREE LOADERS**

title **Music to break a sub-lease**

The 1950s 'mood music' trend, with tunes for reading, loving and partying, soon became something of a joke and titles such as this began to appear. Nevertheless, Don Costa was a producer and arranger for some big names in the 1950s and '60s, including Frank Sinatra.

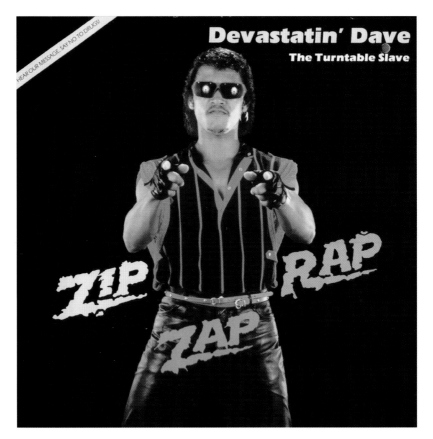

artist **DEVASTATIN' DAVE** THE TURNTABLE SLAVE

title **Zip Zap Rap**

When you choose a look that was cool for just about a month and then combine it with a party-killing anti-drugs message, you are going to struggle for chart recognition. Nevertheless, Dave now performs as 'Devastatin' Dave the Cyberslave' and released *Havin' A Dream* in 2000.

artist **DEBBIE DRAKE**

title **How to Keep your Husband Happy**

Debbie Drake's sexually charged exercise records provided a clear blueprint for the self-conscious repression of the 1950s female. The cover notes helpfully state that 'Fighting against weight is one of the surest ways of fighting for a husband's continued love, and getting it.'

artist **JOYCE DRAKE**
title   *Joyce*

Of all the records on my website, I get the most emails about this 1983 album. Something about Joyce touches people, but I'm not quite sure what it is. To me, she seems to be saying, 'Don't be afraid! Let's get together for coffee before my next hair appointment.'

artist   **DENNIS FARNON AND HIS ORCHESTRA**

title   **Caution! Men Swinging**

Dennis was born in Canada in 1923 and trained as a trumpeter. However, he is best known as the composer of the background music to the 1950s Mr Magoo cartoon series. Here, his eyes draw you in and make you wonder just how many blue-collar guys he's helped to 'swing'.

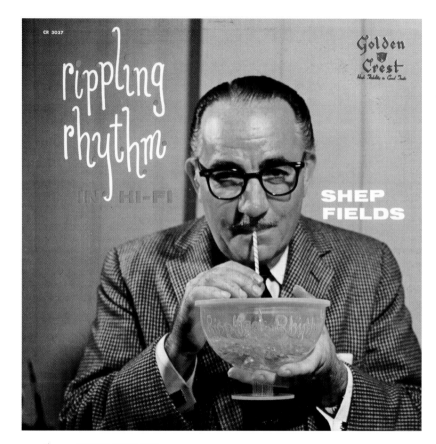

CR 3037

rippling rhythm

IN HI-FI

Golden Crest

SHEP FIELDS

artist **SHEP FIELDS**

title **Rippling Rhythm in Hi-Fi**

Shep Fields and his Rippling Rhythm Orchestra enjoyed moderate success in the 1930s and '40s. Shep would introduce each performance by humming a tune through a straw held in a pot of water, thus demonstrating the musical effect the band strove to produce.

artist **FONTANNA AND HIS ORCHESTRA**

title **Music for Expectant Fathers**

The cover notes sum up this 1957 'mood music' album: 'What the poor expectant father goes through!... So, listen, Daddy-to-be. When you come home after a hard day's work... put this album on... slip into your favourite chair... light your pipe, and listen...'.

artist   **FREDDIE GAGE**

title   **All my friends are dead**

Known as 'The Underworld Preacher', Freddie Gage is a reformed drug addict from Texas. In the 1950s he founded the Pulpit in the Shadows ministry dedicated to 'reaching restless youth... victims of drug abuse, hippies,... the rebel motorcycle gangs, and society dropouts'.

rejoice, dear hearts!
BROTHER DAVE GARDNER

Live, In Person Performance
RCA VICTOR
LPM-2083
A "New Orthophonic" High Fidelity Recording

artist   **BROTHER DAVE GARDNER**

title   **Rejoice, Dear Hearts!**

Brother Dave was not a real preacher; he was in fact a popular comedian in the southern United States during the 1950s and '60s. His sly storytelling style has been compared to that of the novelist Mark Twain. He died of a heart attack in 1983 on a film set.

PRODUCED BY ED PENNEY

MCA-5255

artist   **TERRI GIBBS**

title   **I'm a Lady**

Hailing from Augusta, Georgia, Terri Gibbs, who is blind, enjoyed much success as a country and gospel singer and pianist, and was nominated for a Grammy award in 1987. Terri and her monogrammed glasses, however, have since retired from music.

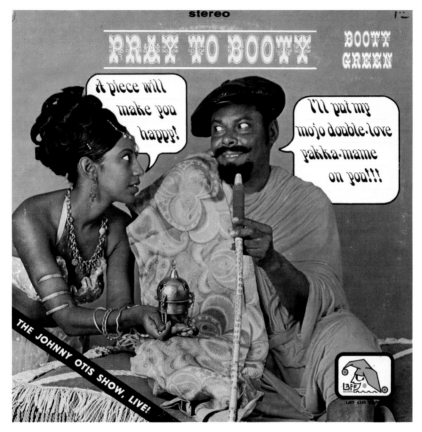

artist **BOOTY GREEN**

title **Pray To Booty**

Laff Records' 1960s series of 'black comedy' records broke all barriers when it came to the album cover – explicit sex, drugs and profanity were the norm. Other titles included *Big Dead Dick* and *Mutha is Half a Word*.

artist **BRUCE HAACK**

title **The Way-Out Record for Children**

Bruce Haack attended New York's prestigious Juilliard School and was an inventor and exponent of synthesizers. He focused his talent on making albums for children, as with this 1968 recording. He is acknowledged by many as a forerunner of modern electronic music.

artist   **MILLIE JACKSON**

title   **Back to the S**t**

Millie Jackson, a controversial R&B artist, has released over 20 albums since 1973. However, her explicit lyrics and lewd album covers have hindered mainstream acceptance of her music. She currently owns a recording studio in Dallas, Texas.

artist **MILLIE JACKSON**

title   **E.S.P. (Extra Sexual Persuasion)**

Millie's brutal honesty and humour is not only evident in her songs but in her interviews as well: when asked by *Rolling Stone* magazine why she released a repetitive second live album, she replied, 'Because you motherf***ers didn't buy the last one!'

artist   **WINDY JOHNSON & THE MESSENGERS**

title   **With You in Mind**

The cover notes to this 1975 recording sum up its message: 'Confusion, disappointments, and difficulties may surround us, but the Messengers remind us we only need to stop and realize these are but passing moments in the aeons of time where God is concerned.'

artist **JONAH JONES**

title **I Dig Chicks**

The pairing of curvaceous models and heavy machinery was fairly popular on 1950s album covers, and these women are certainly defying gravity! Jonah Jones was the star trumpet player in Cab Calloway's band before going solo. He died in 2000 at 91 years of age.

artist **TYLER KING AND THE TWISTEENS**

title **Twistin' Time**

The enthusiastic cover notes state that 'adults from Maine to California (and in England and France, too, for that matter), have been brought into the fold through a new dance craze that is sweeping the world... It is called the "Twist".'

artist   **J. MARTIN KOHE**

title   **How to Overcome Discouragement**

The depressing style of this Success Motivation Institute cover even continues into the cover notes, which bizarrely encourage you to accept your discouragement, 'make it a part of your life, and face the happy future that awaits you'... What future?

Signature ✳
SM 1003

the
garden of
❊eddie
lawrence

artist   **EDDIE LAWRENCE**

title   **The Garden of Eddie Lawrence**

Belying the creepy nature of this album cover, which seems to be aimed at enticing innocents into Eddie's garden, Eddie was actually a comedian who had a big hit in 1956 with the song *The Old Philosopher*.

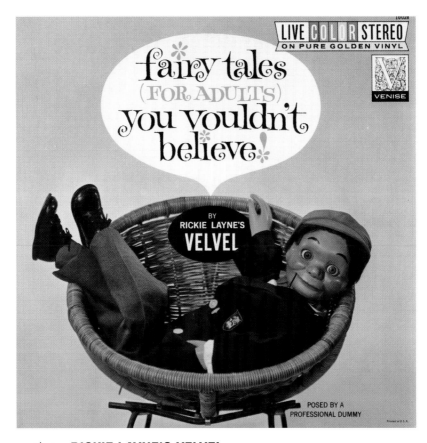

artist **RICKIE LAYNE'S VELVEL**

title **Fairy Tales (for Adults) You Vouldn't Believe**

Comedian Rickie Layne and his sidekick, a ventriloquist's dummy called Velvel, were regulars on *The Ed Sullivan Show* in the late 1950s. In an era when many comedians capitalized on racial and ethnic stereotypes, Velvel spoke with a strong Jewish accent.

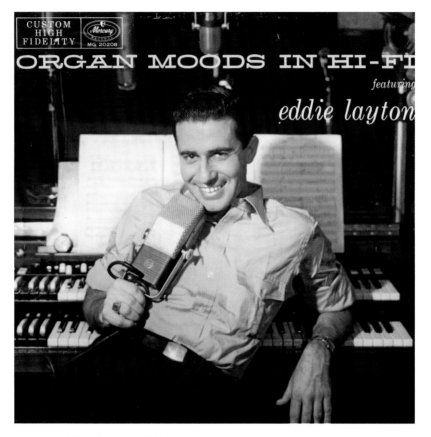

CUSTOM
HIGH
FIDELITY

Mercury
RECORDS
MG 20208

ORGAN MOODS IN HI-FI

featuring

eddie layton

artist **EDDIE LAYTON**
title   **Organ Moods in Hi-Fi**

Finding subtle sexual subtext in an organ-themed album cover is not unusual. Mr Layton, however, does not seem to believe in subtlety! This example demonstrates how a well-placed microphone can easily liven up a dull album cover.

MERCURY · GREAT ORGAN HITS · EDDIE LAYTON AT THE HAMMOND ORGAN

SR 60639

MERCURY STEREO

Mercury RECORDS

★ GREAT ★ ORGAN HITS

★ BY THE WATERS OF THE MINNETONKA
★ AIN'T MISBEHAVIN'
★ THE HAPPY ORGAN
★ THE PERFECT SONG
★ TWILIGHT TIME
★ YOU CAN'T BE TRUE, DEAR
★ GRANADA
★ THE DIPSY DOODLE
★ MR. LUCKY
★ TICO TICO
★ WHEN THE ORGAN PLAYED AT TWILIGHT
★ PATRICIA

Eddie Layton
at the
Hammond Organ

artist **EDDIE LAYTON**

title **Great Organ Hits**

Eddie demonstrated Hammond organs before beginning his recording career, and perhaps the Freudian touches seen on his album covers were a trick he learnt as a salesman. For 25 years, Eddie was also the official organist for the Yankee Stadium and the New York Yankees.

songs of couch and consultation

- shrinker man
- the will to fail
- the guilty rag
- stay as sick as you are
- hush little sibling
- real sick sounds
- repressed hostility blues
- i can't get adjusted to the you who got adjusted to me
- schizophrenic moon
- properly loved
- gunslinger, (a ballad for adult westerns)
- it must be something psychological

sung by katie lee

artist **KATIE LEE**

title **Songs of couch and consultation**

Song titles on this therapeutic album by the glamorous Katie Lee include *Repressed Hostility Blues*, *I Can't Get Adjusted to the You Who Got Adjusted to Me*, *Schizophrenic Moon*, *The Will to Fail* and *Real Sick Sounds*. Enough said.

artist **LITTLE JOE AND THE LATINAIRES**

title *Mas!!! Arriba*

In the late 1960s everyone got into the outer-space craze. This cover shows that Little Joe was modern, patriotic and maybe just a little 'out there'! He knew what he was doing, however, as by 2003 he had released over 50 albums and been nominated for four Grammy Awards.

artist **LIVING MARIMBAS**

title **Mexican Joe and Other Favorites**

A music lover visiting Mexico in the 1960s might have been surprised to find that not everyone was always fully armed. Living Marimbas were part of RCA's 'Living' series of groups, along with the likes of Living Guitars, Living Percussion, Living Jazz and, best of all, Living Organs.

FEATURING
MUSIC BY LORIN-
FRANK PRODUCTIONS
COMPOSED AND ARRANGED
BY WILL LORIN

SOUND TRACK RECORDING
FROM *GE* TRUE

MUSIC TO DRILL OIL WELLS BY

artist **WILL LORIN AND LORIN-FRANK PRODUCTIONS**
title **Music to Drill Oil Wells By**

With the popularity of 'mood music' albums, corporate America was quick to jump on the bandwagon. In addition to this gem from General Electric, there were such unlikely titles as *Music To Shave By* (Remington razors) and *Music To Eat Pizza By* (Jeno's Pizza).

artist **SHARRON L. LUCKY**

title **Carpet Square**

The cover notes do little to explain this bizarre album: 'The stimulation of the student's creativity is a feature of "Carpet Square". Standing on carpet square (nap down), student does twisting motion which propels him across the floor… Shag carpet is not recommended.'

HIFI RECORD

TABOO VOL. 2

NEW EXOTIC SOUNDS OF ARTHUR LYMAN

artist **ARTHUR LYMAN**

title **Taboo Vol. 2: New Exotic Sounds of Arthur Lyman**

Arthur Lyman was one of the undisputed masters of 'exotica': music that consisted of lush string and percussion arrangements spiced up with monkey calls and macaw shrieks. His album covers were always exciting, usually featuring blasting volcanoes or other explosive fare.

artist **THE MASTER'S FOUR**

title **Because of God's Love**

These *five* dapper charmers – they obviously couldn't count – hailed from Dallas, Texas. The Master's Four are C.T. Laird, Samuel Ray, Harmen McKenzie, Clayton Northcutt and David Kaps. We can only wonder what they are all looking at so animatedly.

A **SINGER** *Christmas for the family*

WHITE CHRISTMAS
O COME ALL YE FAITHFUL
JOY TO THE WORLD
DECK THE HALLS
O HOLY NIGHT
SILENT NIGHT
THE FIRST NOEL
O LITTLE TOWN OF BETHLEHEM
AWAY IN A MANGER
HARK! THE HERALD ANGELS SING
GOD REST YE MERRY GENTLEMEN
WE WISH YOU A MERRY CHRISTMAS

THE MASTERTONE ORCHESTRA
featuring
THE DON JANSE CHORALE

*A Trademark of THE SINGER COMPANY.

artist **THE MASTERTONE ORCHESTRA FEATURING THE DON JANSE CHORALE**

title **A Singer Christmas for the Family**

This 1963 album manages to strip the festive season of all the traditional trappings, but thank goodness for the sewing machine – at least bemused Mum can make all the family some presents.

The McKeithen's

Featuring
Praise...
Im Gonna Tarry
Give It All To...

artist **THE McKEITHENS**

title **The McKeithens**

Style in the 1970s was all about hair and, while hippies opted for the natural, unwashed look, the Christian lady chose size. Well, someone did once say, 'The bigger the hair, the closer to God', which makes Mrs McKeithen well on her way to meeting the great hairstylist in the sky!

artist **THE MEEKS FAMILY**

title **New Jerusalem's Where I'm Bound**

Many religious 'family' records, among them this album by the Meeks Family, proudly feature the motorhome or trailer in which the group would travel the country to perform their act at churches and revivals.

ⓔⓢⓒ RECORD · 121 ·   A PRODUCT OF PIP RECORDS

artist **DR GEORGE MILSTEIN**

title **Music to Grow Plants**

Dr George Milstein, an avid gardener, discovered that constant exposure to a hum with a frequency of 3,000 cycles per second greatly increased the growth rate of plants. In this record he mixed the hum with easy-listening music for the benefit of both listener and plants.

SANTA CLAUS IS COMIN'
TO TOWN
WHITE CHRISTMAS
HERE COMES SANTA CLAUS
RUDOLPH THE RED-NOSED
REINDEER
I SAW MOMMY KISSING
SANTA CLAUS
SILVER BELLS

artist **THE MOM AND DADS**

title **Merry Christmas with The Mom and Dads**

Ah, that's more like it! An authentic and traditional Christmas, except that there are three fathers and just one mother! So, which lucky fella scored with the lovely gift of polyester? This band specializes in polka music and is particularly popular in Canada and Australia.

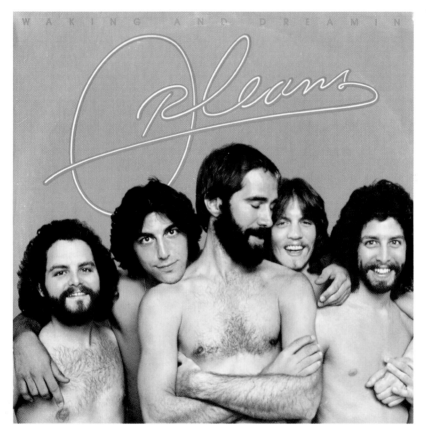

WAKING AND DREAMIN

artist **ORLEANS**

title **Waking and Dreaming**

The rock band Orleans formed in upstate New York in 1972. This 'revealing' 1976 album contains their classic hit, *Still The One*. The band toured (clothed) with Fleetwood Mac and REO Speedwagon in 1995 and released a 30th anniversary live album in 2002.

artist **KORLA PANDIT**

title **Merry Xmas**

Korla Pandit was born John Roland Redd in Missouri. He moved to California in the 1940s, where he developed the character of a dreamy-eyed Indian organist and soon became a television star. He appeared as himself in Tim Burton's movie *Ed Wood*.

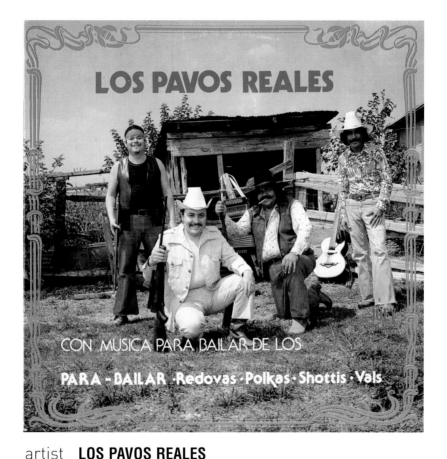

artist **LOS PAVOS REALES**

title **Para-Bailar Redovas Polkas Shottis Vals**

Sometimes I find an album cover that completely baffles me. What are these fellows getting ready for? A hunting trip? A gig? A visit to the moustache trimmers? Whatever, Los Pavos Reales, aka The Peacocks, have been releasing records since 1964.

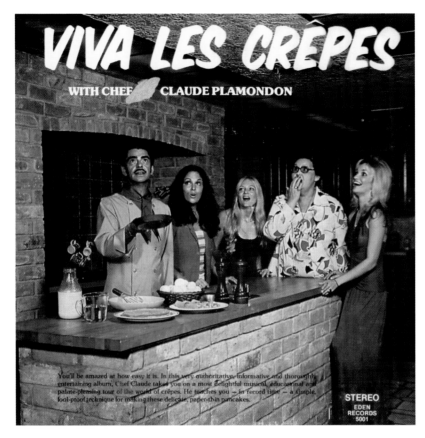

VIVA LES CRÊPES

WITH CHEF CLAUDE PLAMONDON

You'll be amazed at how easy it is. In this very authoritative, informative and thoroughly entertaining album, Chef Claude takes you on a most delightful musical, educational and palate-pleasing tour of the world of crêpes. He teaches you – in record time – a simple, fool-proof technique for making these delicate, paper-thin pancakes.

STEREO
EDEN
RECORDS
5001

artist   **CHEF CLAUDE PLAMONDON**

title   **Viva Les Crêpes**

From the sleeve notes: '[Plamondon's] livelihood is not preparing an excellent crêpe... His real talent lies in seeking that one vulnerable spot in us... Don't mistake this album as just a 1,2,3 course in learning to make crêpes; it can be a very warm human experience shared.'

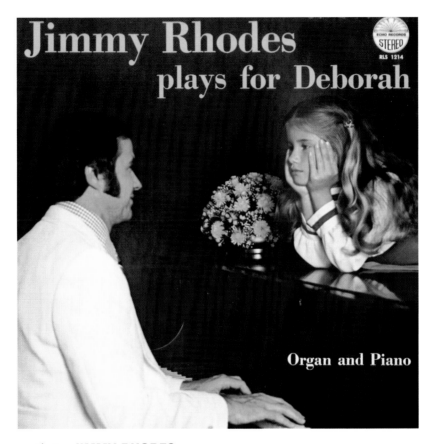

Jimmy Rhodes
plays for Deborah

ECHO RECORDS
STEREO
RLS 1214

Organ and Piano

artist **JIMMY RHODES**

title **Jimmy Rhodes Plays For Deborah**

One would hope a young girl would have better things to do than lounge around on a piano, gazing blankly into her daddy's eyes. I wonder what the adult Deborah now thinks about her bored appearance on this 'classic' record.

artist **THE SINGING RICHEY FAMILY**

title **Leavin' My Troubles**

OK, people, now we really *are* talking HAIR. This 1976 album's cover notes proudly declare the Richey family's patriotism, perhaps in an attempt to dismiss the idea that Mrs Richey may have been transmitting signals to America's enemies from within her bouffant.

artist   **THE RITCHIE FAMILY**
title   **Bad Reputation**

The Ritchie Family were created by producers Ritchie Rome and Jacques Morali, who later created the Village People. None of the members of the all-female group pictured on the cover to this 1979 album were related to each other or even named Ritchie.

artist **LULU ROMAN**
title **Now Let Me Sing**

LuLu was a regular cast member of the *Hee Haw* television show for over 25 years and performed at President Ronald Reagan's inauguration in 1980. She has recently written a cookbook and has a line of gourmet snacks called 'LuLu Roman's Parlor Treats'.

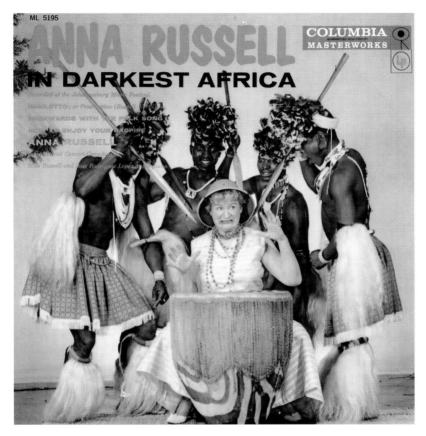

artist **ANNA RUSSELL**

title **In Darkest Africa**

This one is definitely a bad album cover all-time classic! The 'natives', appropriately clad in tablecloths and Pomeranians, seem to be just moments away from sending Ms Russell to the cookpot on a skewer. I guess she shouldn't have messed with their drum!

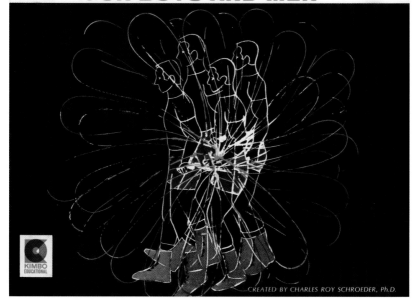

LP1132

Rope Jumping

FOR BOYS AND MEN

CREATED BY CHARLES ROY SCHROEDER, Ph.D.

artist   **CHARLES ROY SCHROEDER, Ph.D.**

title   **Rope Jumping for Boys and Men**

In the United States in the 1970s there was an entire industry of 'gym class' records to be played during the school exercise period. Most of them seem aimed more towards keeping a class full of restless kids busy for an hour than at promoting healthy exercise.

The
Singing Midget
Lowell Mason
and the Crusaders

Crusade
LPM 4202

SING

FOR GOD

AND

COUNTRY

artist   **THE SINGING MIDGET LOWELL MASON AND THE CRUSADERS**
title   **Sing for God and Country**

Many artists were unafraid to make a gimmick out of themselves to sell records, and this album's cover notes suggest that Lowell Mason certainly traded on his stature: 'Because of his unique size, winning personality and singing ability, he is in great demand…'.

artist   **JOHN AND GARY SMITH**

title   **From Show Business to God's Business**

One of the most important decisions when designing an album is the location for the cover shoot. Some choose the beauty of a natural landscape, the hustle and bustle of a city or the controlled environment of a studio; others just choose the nearest car park!

artist **SNEAKERS & LACE**

title **Skateboardin' USA**

When the sport of surfing came out of the water and hit the streets, all imagination seems to have been lost, as seen from some of the song titles on this lost gem from 1978: *Skateboardin'*, *Skateboardin' USA* and *Little Skateboard Queen*.

artist   **SONGS OF FAITH**

title   **Press On**

If you are ever mugged by a man in a purple tuxedo next to a waterfall in a forest and can't remember whether he had a beard or not, this is what the police line-up might look like!

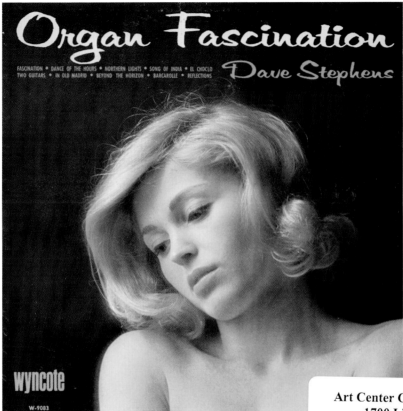

artist **DAVE STEPHENS**

title *Organic Fascination*

Organ Fascination

If you didn't know any better you might have thought this album should have been entitled 'Organ Disappointment' from the look on the cover model's face. However, you knew that it was an album of organ music, of course.

artist **SWAMP DOGG**

title **Rat On!**

Swamp Dogg, aka Jerry Williams, Jr, is an R&B singer and songwriter known for his sometimes odd and humorous lyrics. He has recorded many albums in his 40-year career, including this 1971 offering, but he has never achieved the mainstream popularity some think he deserves.

artist **TONY TEE**

title **Time To Get Physical**

In the days before rappers were corporate moneymakers, their low-budget attempts at album covers often had hilarious results. As Tony Tee demonstrates on the cover of this 1988 recording, one should always use 'spotters' when 'gettin' it on' on the weight bench!

FINGERLESS FIDDLER

Roy Thackerson

VOLUMN I
STEREO

artist **ROY THACKERSON**
title **Fingerless Fiddler**

In 1944, six-year-old Roy found a dynamite cap on the ground and decided to light it. The resulting explosion left him blind in one eye and severely maimed his left hand. In 1968 Roy devised a device to allow him to hold and play a fiddle. He still performs regularly.

ZLP 664

Marcy SINGS TO Children

$1.98

I'LL BE A SUNBEAM • WHEN MR. SATAN KNOCKS AT MY HEART'S DOOR • CLIMB, CLIMB UP SUNSHINE MOUNTAIN
"OH" • THERE IS SOMETHING YOU CAN DO • WHY WORRY WHEN YOU CAN PRAY? • I'M IN THE LORD'S ARMY

JESUS LOVES ME • THE WINDOW'S OF HEAVEN ARE OPEN • HOW DID MOSES CROSS THE RED SEA?
YOU'LL ALWAYS BE HAPPY • SOMEWHERE BEYOND THE BLUE • A-B-C-D-E-F-G • WHISPER A PRAYER

ZONDERVAN
RECORDINGS

artist **MARCY TIGNER**

title **Marcy Sings to Children**

Marcy Tigner was an aspiring gospel singer whose career was stymied by her high, childlike voice. She finally found fame after learning ventriloquism and inventing her 'Little Marcy' character. She released dozens of records in the 1960s and '70s and was wildly successful.

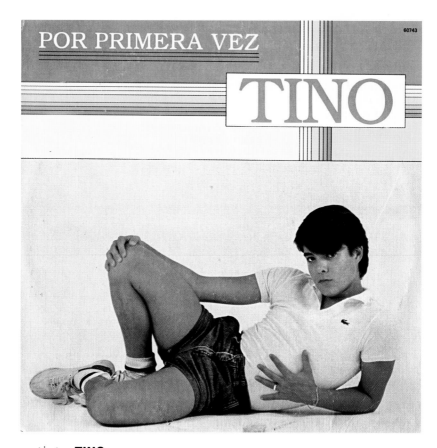

artist **TINO**

title **Por Primera Vez**

Tino (Constantino Fernandez) was a member of the popular Spanish kids' group Parchis. Their first international hit was a cover version of the Village People's *In the Navy* and, if this album cover is any indication, Tino would have had a wide appeal.

artist   **UNFOLDING**

title   **How to Blow Your Mind and Have a Freak-out Party**

The sleeve notes explain this 1967 album: 'Put a rock and roll record on the phonograph… point [a] kaleidescope [sic] at the TV screen… Now play the record at a different speed. YOU ARE NOW FREAKING OUT.'

artist **VARGAS DE TECALITLAN**

title **15 Grandes de El Mariachi**

Cockfighting is an ancient sport. England banned the cockfight in 1849 and all US states except New Mexico and Louisiana have outlawed the practice. However, the 'sport of kings' is still popular and legal elsewhere, including Mexico, where this group comes from.

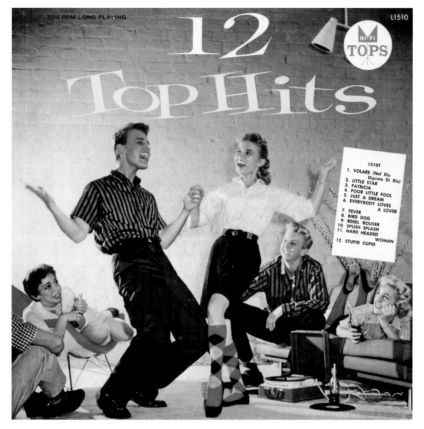

artist   **VARIOUS ARTISTS**

title   **12 Top Hits**

Tops was one of the largest budget record labels of the 1950s and '60s. They produced musical selections usually recorded by nameless studio musicians and sold in discount stores. A great album cover was thought to make up for the sub-standard quality of the music!

CSP 244

SOUND OFF...SOFTLY

FROM THE MAKERS OF GOLD BOND CEILING TILE...RICH MUSIC IN HI-FI FOR YOUR LISTENING PLEASURE

LES & LARRY ELGART / BASIE-ELLINGTON / LES BROWN / PERCY FAITH / SAUL GOODMAN / TONY BENNETT / PATTI PAGE / GORDON JENKINS / RAY CONNIFF / BOBBY HACKETT / ANDRE KOSTELANETZ

artist **VARIOUS ARTISTS**

title **Sound Off... Softly**

The cover notes explain this recording, which comes from the makers of ceiling tiles: 'Unfortunately, today's trends... produce rooms with far less than good acoustics... Echoes... can make an utter hash out of what started out as good music. What is needed is... ceiling tile.'

NANCY WALKER
I HATE MEN
SID BASS AND HIS ORCHESTRA
I'm Gonna Wash That Man Right Outa My Hair
Boy! What Love Has Done to Me!
Ev'rything I've Got
I Hate Men
Most Gentlemen Don't Like Love
Take Him
To Keep My Love Alive
What Is a Man?
Without You
You Irritate Me So

RCA CAMDEN

CAL 561 A "New Orthophonic" High Fidelity Recording

artist **NANCY WALKER**
title **I Hate Men**

Poor Nancy... some man's done her an injustice and now she wants to take out her anger on all men. Some inspired titles from the record include *You Irritate Me So*, *Take Him* and the old favourite *I'm Gonna Wash That Man Right Outa My Hair*.

Elmer Wheeler's AWARD WINNING TALK

Selling the Sizzle

SUCCESS MOTIVATION INSTITUTE, INC. ™

TRADE MARK OF SUCCESS MOTIVATION INSTITUTE, INC.

THIS TALK HAS BEEN GIVEN 6,000 TIMES TO MORE THAN 2 MILLION PEOPLE

artist **ELMER WHEELER**

title **Selling the Sizzle**

Elmer Wheeler was the king of celebrity salesmen in the 1950s and '60s. His 'Wheeler Word Lab' tested thousands of words and phrases to find those that generated the most sales. His 'Don't sell the steak, sell the sizzle' philosophy certainly sold thousands of records.

Student Nurses
Sing The Season In

BMC5071

WHIDDEN MEMORIAL
HOSPITAL
EVERETT, MASSACHUSETTS

artist **WHIDDEN MEMORIAL HOSPITAL SCHOOL OF NURSING GLEE CLUB**

title **Student Nurses Sing the Season In**

There are a surprising number of records featuring 'singing nurses' in existence. Perhaps a reason for this can be inferred by this record's cover notes: 'to call attention to the aesthetic qualities of youth…'.

Stereo

AARON WILBURN
HAS ARRIVED!

Nancy L. Orcutt

Har-1007-LP

artist **AARON WILBURN**

title **Aaron Wilburn Has Arrived!**

Aaron Wilburn broke out of his shell at an early age and is still on the scene today. He currently has a Christian comedy routine, performs up to 150 times per year and records new albums. His latest hit was entitled, *If My Nose Was Running Money, I'd Blow It All Over You*.

artist   **JOHN & VICKIJO WITTY**

title   **Family Portrait**

The Wittys are a Christian comedy team that has been performing since 1972. In the 1980s they had a radio show entitled, *The John and VickiJo Witty Five-Minute Blurp. Family Portrait* was released in 1980. The Wittys still perform in churches across the United States.

artist **FRANKIE YANKOVIC**

title **Dance Little Bird**

Frankie Yankovic, known as 'America's polka king', helped popularize polka music, beginning with his first record in 1948. Gimmicky records such as this were advertised on TV and aimed at an undiscerning audience – sounds like my kind of record!

artist **OSCAR ZAMORA** Y **DON CHEMA**

title **El Padrecito**

Oscar Zamora and Don Chema are a Spanish-language 'adult' ventriloquist act, hence the woman being chased. Puppets are a common feature of popular culture in Latin America and can be seen on television game shows, political satires and even news programmes.

Songs That Mom and Dad Taught Us

STEREO

THE FRIENDS

STEREO

artist **THE FRIENDS**

title **Songs That Mom and Dad Taught Us**

This rather confusing cover leads us to wonder whether these two (very) old friends, happy together in their nursing home, are the artists, or whether they are Mom and Dad. Whatever, just absorb their happy vibes and enjoy a singalong.

artist   **NO ARTIST ACCREDITED**

title   **Songs for Swinging Mothers**

This 1962 'record' is a joke sleeve that contained a cardboard disc saying 'I bought this album for you as a gift… sorry, I couldn't afford the record!' Its 'songlist' included *Get Me to the Church on Time*, *This Could Be the Start of Something Big* and *I've Got You Under My Skin*.

Further Information

More Forgotten Records

The author's website:
www.bizarrerecords.com

Show and tell music:
www.showandtellmusic.com

David Letterman:
www.cbs.com/latenight/lateshow/
exclusives/record_collection/

Record label discographies:
www.bsnpubs.com/discog

Artists' Websites

Gary Dee Bradford:
www.garybradfordmusic.com

Max Bygraves:
www.maxbygraves.co.uk

Bruce Haack:
www.brucehaack.com

Millie Jackson:
www.weirdwreckuds.com

Little Joe:
www.littlejoeylafamilia.homestead.com

Arthur Lyman:
www.arthurlyman.com

Orleans:
www.orleansmusic.com

Korla Pandit:
www.korlapandit.com

LuLu Roman:
www.luluroman.20m.com

Success Motivation Institute:
www.success-motivation.com

Swamp Dogg:
www.swampdogg.com

Roy Thackerson:
www.fingerlessfiddler.com

Aaron Wilburn:
www.aaronwilburn.com

Frankie Yankovic:
www.polkas.com/yankovic

Picture Acknowledgements

All album covers are from the author's collection except the following:

Pages 23, 27, 37, 38, 43, 44, 49, 54, 62, 73, 82, 85, 87
which are all from the collection of John Spath.

The Publishers would like to thank all artists and recording companies who agreed to be included in the book. Every effort was made to contact the parties concerned with the copyright of these album covers.

Author Acknowledgements

Special thanks to Allison Bale for finding so many of these records for me!
    Thanks also to Jon Spath, Andy Wright, Matt Murillo and everyone else who has discovered records for me over the years.

First published in 2004 by New Holland Publishers (UK) Ltd
London · Cape Town · Sydney · Auckland

www.newhollandpublishers.com

Garfield House, 86–88 Edgware Road, London W2 2EA, United Kingdom

80 McKenzie Street, Cape Town 8001, South Africa

14 Aquatic Drive, Frenchs Forest, NSW 2086, Australia

218 Lake Road, Northcote, Auckland, New Zealand

10 9 8 7 6 5 4 3 2 1

ISBN 1 84330 888 6

Publishing Manager: Jo Hemmings
Senior Editor: Kate Michell
Editor: Sarah Larter
Assistant Editor: Rose Hudson
Cover Design and Design: Gülen Shevki-Taylor
Production: Joan Woodroffe

Reproduction by Modern Age Repro House Ltd, Hong Kong
Printed and bound by Craft Print International Pte Ltd, Singapore

Publisher's Note:
Every effort has been made to contact the parties concerned with the copyright of these album covers. Any further information pertaining to copyright will be included in future editions.